Idea for this book by Bettina Schipp & Reynhard Boegl.
Book layout & design by kick-image.at
Photos: privat
© 2024 by B. Schipp & R. Boegl, www.songbooks.info

PLAY UKULELE DUETS
UKULELE & BARITONE UKULELE

30 Weihnachtslieder / Christmas Songs

www.songbooks.info

Inhaltsverzeichnis / table of content

Die Ukulele / the Ukulele 6

Stimmung / tuning 6

Tabulaturerklärung / explanation of the tab........................7

Alle Jahre wieder 8

Am Weihnachtsbaum die Lichter brennen 9

Angels we have heard on high 10

Away in a manger 12

Christmas is coming..14

Der Christbaum ist der schönste Baum 16

Es ist ein Ros' entsprungen 18

Es wird scho glei dumpa 20

Fröhliche Weihnacht...22

God rest ye merry, Gentleman 24

Go, tell it on the mountain 26

Hark! The Herald Angels sing..28

Ihr Kinderlein kommet..30

I saw three ships...32

SOUNDS - ONLINE...33

Jingle Bells 34

Lasst uns froh und munter sein 37

Josef, lieber Josef mein...38

Kommet, ihr Hirten 40

Leise rieselt der Schnee 42

Maria durch ein Dornwald ging 44

Morgen, Kinder, wirds was geben.................................45

Morgen kommt der Weihnachtsmann................................46

O Tannenbaum 47

O come, all ye faithful..48

O du fröhliche 50

Stille Nacht 52

The first Noel 54

Schneeflöckchen, Weißröckchen 56

Vom Himmel hoch, da komm ich her 57

We wish you a marry christmas.....................................58

Die Ukulele / the Ukulele

Viele Legenden ranken sich um die Namensgebung der Ukulele, deren Geschichte bis ins Jahr 1879 zurückreicht. In diesem Jahr soll es auch gewesen sein, als sich ein junges, hübsches Mädchen eine Braguinha (ein portugiesisches, kleines Saiteninstrument) borgte und so flink darauf spielte, dass alle Zuhörer diese lustige Darbietung mit einem „hüpfenden Floh" verglichen.

Mit der Zeit veränderte sich dieses portugiesische Saiteninstrument – der Name jedoch blieb: „hüpfender Floh". oder auf Hawaiianisch: Ukulele.

Many legends tell about the naming of the ukulele, its history dates back to 1879. In this year, a pretty young girl borrowed a Braguinha (a small string instrument from Portugal) and played so fast on it, that all listeners compared this funny performance with a „jumping flea".

Over time, this portuguese string instrument changed - but the name remained the same: „jumping flea" or Hawaiian: Ukulele.

Stimmung / tuning

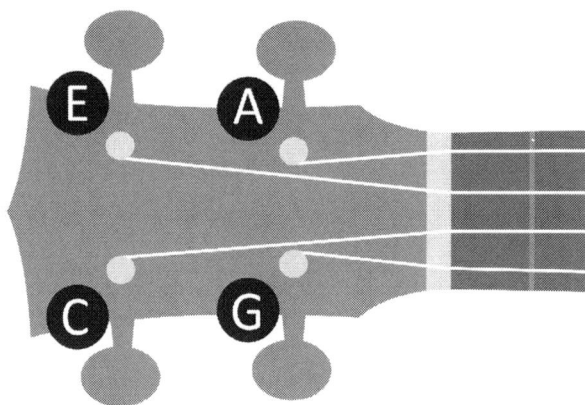

Ukulele
In traditioneller hawaiianische Stimmung
in traditional hawaiian tuning

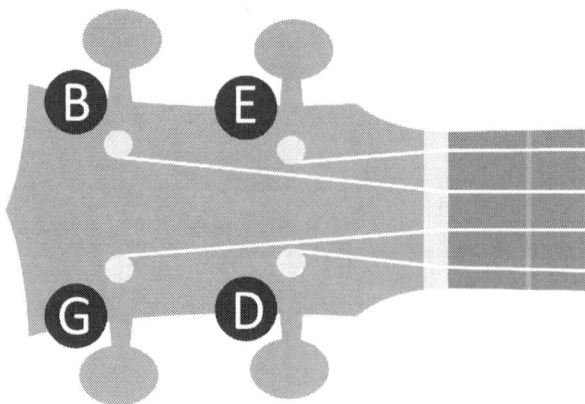

Bariton Ukulele

Tabulaturerklärung / explanation of the tab

1 1/16 Note - 4 Töne pro Schlag
1/16 note - 4 notes per beat

2 1/4 Note - 1 Ton pro Schlag
1/4 note - 1 note per beat

3 1/8 Noten - 2 Töne pro Schlag
1/8 notes - 2 notes per beat

4 Taktstrich
Barline

5 Triole - 3 Töne pro Schlag
Triplet - 3 tones per beat

6 „punktierter" Notenwert - um die Hälfte länger
„Dotted" note value - longer by half

7 halbe Note - 2 Schläge lang
half note - 2 beats long

8 1/1 Pause - ein Takt lang
1/1 rest - one bar long

9 1/2 Pause - 2 Schläge lang
1/2 rest - 2 beats long

10 1/4 Pause - 1 Schlag lang
1/4 rest - 1 beat long

11 1/8 Pause - 1/2 Schlag lang
1/8 rest - 1/2 beat long

Die Zahlen auf den vier Linien („Saiten") geben den Bund an, der gegriffen wird.

The numbers on the four lines („strings") indicate the fret that is gripped.

www.songbooks.info

Alle Jahre wieder

Beat: 4/4

F. Silcher, W. Hey

Al – le Jah – re   wie – der   kommt da – s Chris – tus – kind.

Auf die Er – de   nie – de – r   wo wir   Men – schen – sind.

Am Weihnachtsbaum die Lichter brennen

Beat: 3/4

Traditional, H. Kletke

Ukulele

Am Weih-nachts – baum die – Lich-ter bren – nen, wie glänzt er

Bariton Ukulele

fest – lich, lieb und mild. Als spräch' er: "Wollt' ihr in mir er –

ken – nen ge – treu – er Hoff – nung, stil – les Bild."

Angels we have heard on high

Beat: 4/4

Traditional

Lyrics:

An-gels we have heard onhigh, sweet-ly sing-ing o'er theplains.

And the moun-tains in re-ply, ech-o-ing their joy-ousstrains.

Glo - o-o-o-o - o - o-o-o-o - o - o-o-o-o - o - ri-a

G   D   G   C   G   D   G   Em   Am   D

13

in ex – cel – sis De – o,   Glo – o-o-o-o – o – o-o-o-o

G   C   D7   G   D   G   C   G   D7

17

o – o-o-o-o – o – ri – a,   in ex – cel – sis De –

G

21

o.

Away in a manger

Beat: 3/4

Traditional

Ukulele

A - way in a man - ger, no crib for a bed. The

Bariton Ukulele

lit - tle Lord Je - sus laid down his sweet head. The

stars in the sk - y looked down where he lay. The

14

D			G			Am	D7	G

```
T  3----2----0----    2----0----    0--------------    3----
A  ----------------    ----------    0----0----2----    2----
B  2---------------    0--------0    0---------2----    ----
```


lit – tle   Lord   Jes – us   a –   sleep   on   the   hey.

```
T  ----------------    ------------    ------------    0----
A  ----------------    ----0-------    ----2----2-    0----
B  0----4----0-----    0---------0    2----------    ----
```

Christmas is coming

Beat: 4/4

Traditional

Christ - mas is com - ing, the goose is gett - ing fat.

Please, put a pen - ny in the old man's hat. If you

have - n't got a pen - ny, a ha' pen - ny will do, if you

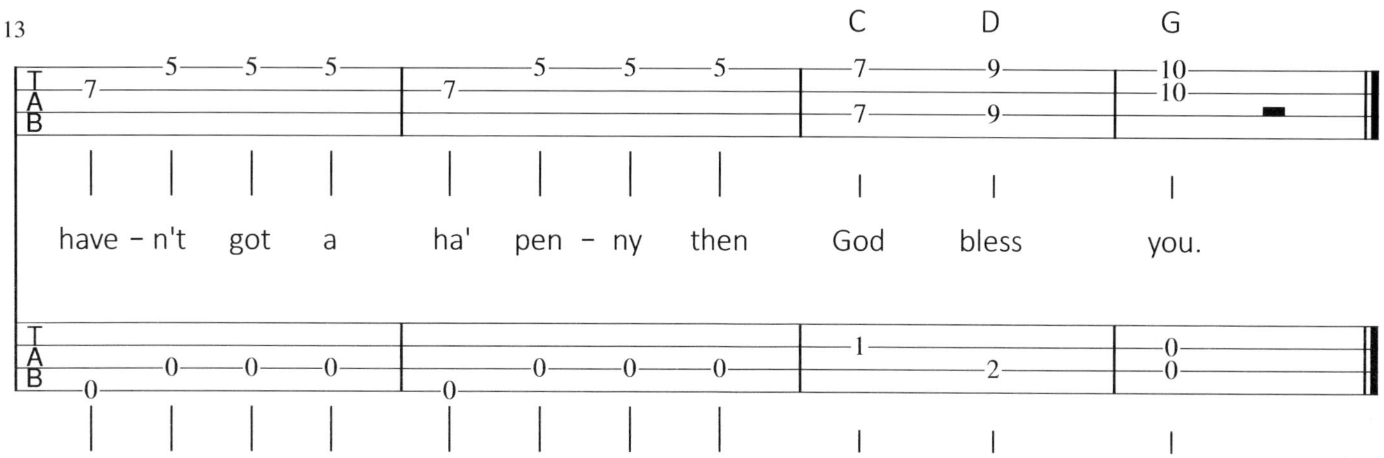
13
C D G
have - n't got a ha' pen - ny then God bless you.

Der Christbaum ist der schöneste Baum

Beat: 4/4

G. Eisenbach

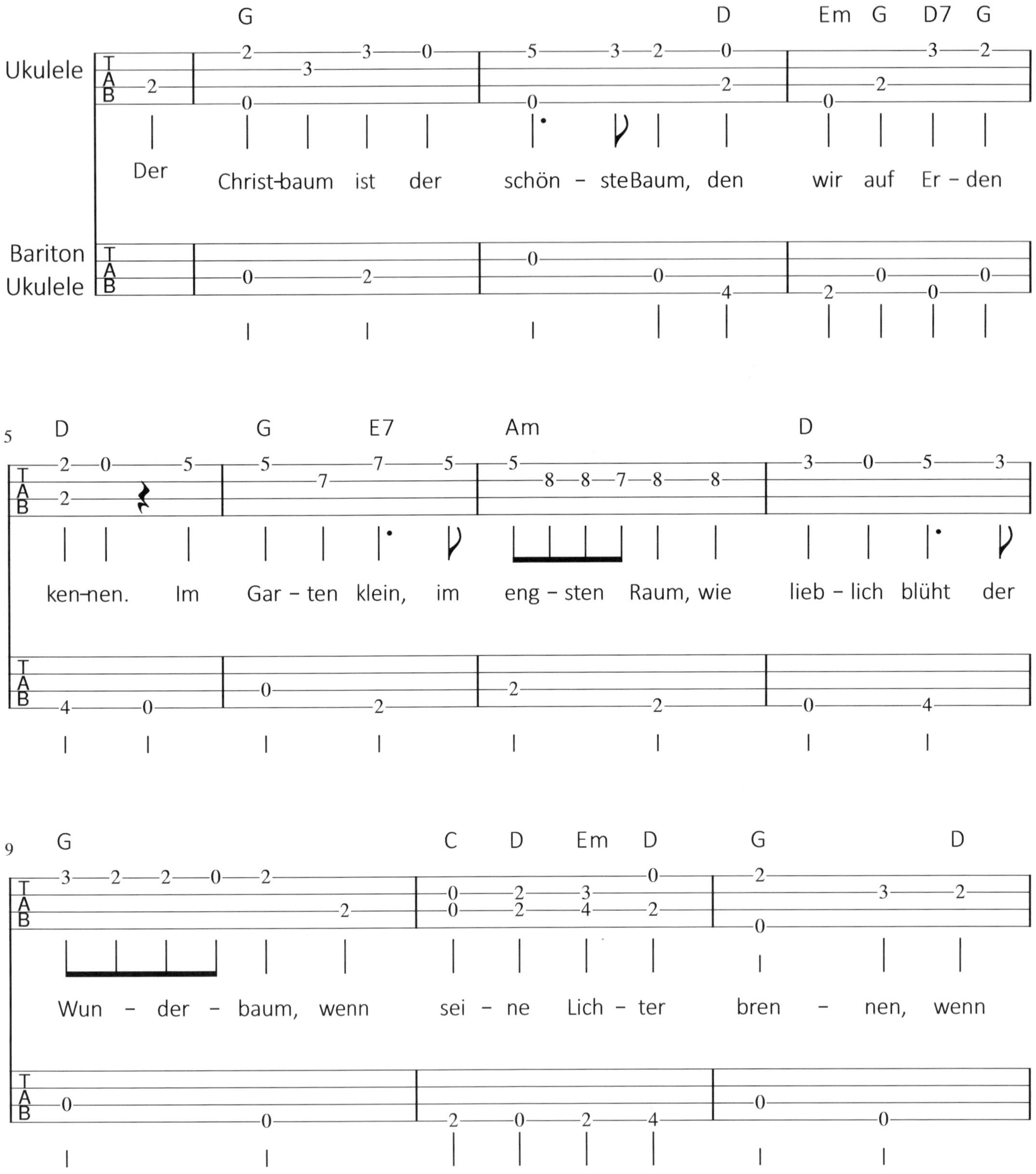

sei – ne   Lich – ter   bren – nen,   ja   bren –   nen.

Es ist ein Ros' entsprungen

Beat: 4/4

M. Praetorius, F. Layriz

Es ist ein Ros' ent-sprun – gen aus ei – ner Wur –

zel zart. Wie uns die Al – ten sun – gen von

Jes – se kam die Art. Und hat ein Blüm – lein 'bracht.

13
G D G C G D Em Am G D G D G
Mit-ten im kal-ten Win - ter wohl zu der hal - benNacht.

Es wird scho glei dumpa

Beat: 3/4

Traditional

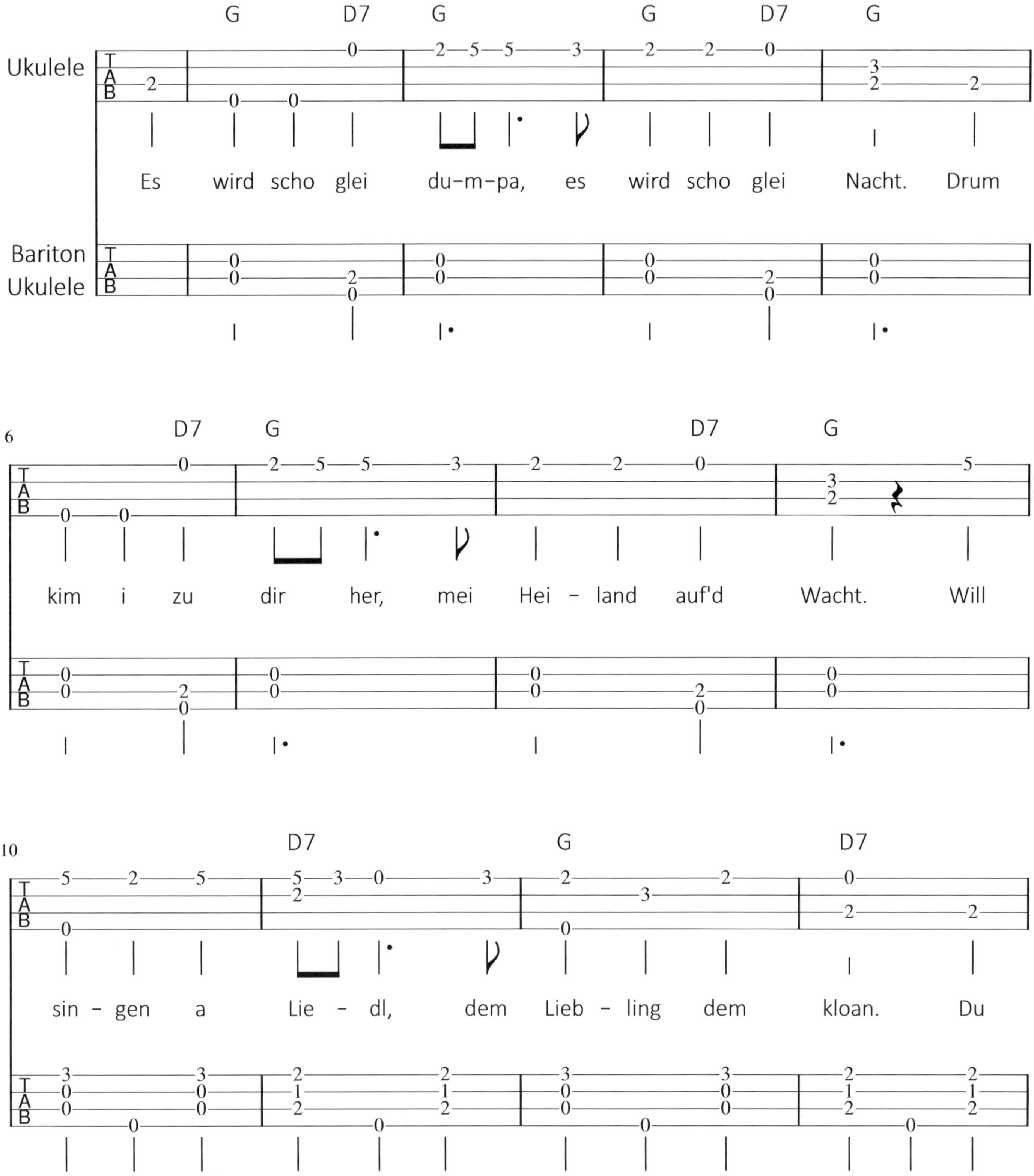

magst ja net schl – a – fn, i hör die nur woan. Hei –

hei, hei – hei, schl–af siaß, Her – z – lia – bs Kind.

Fröhliche Weihnacht

Beat: 4/4

Traditional

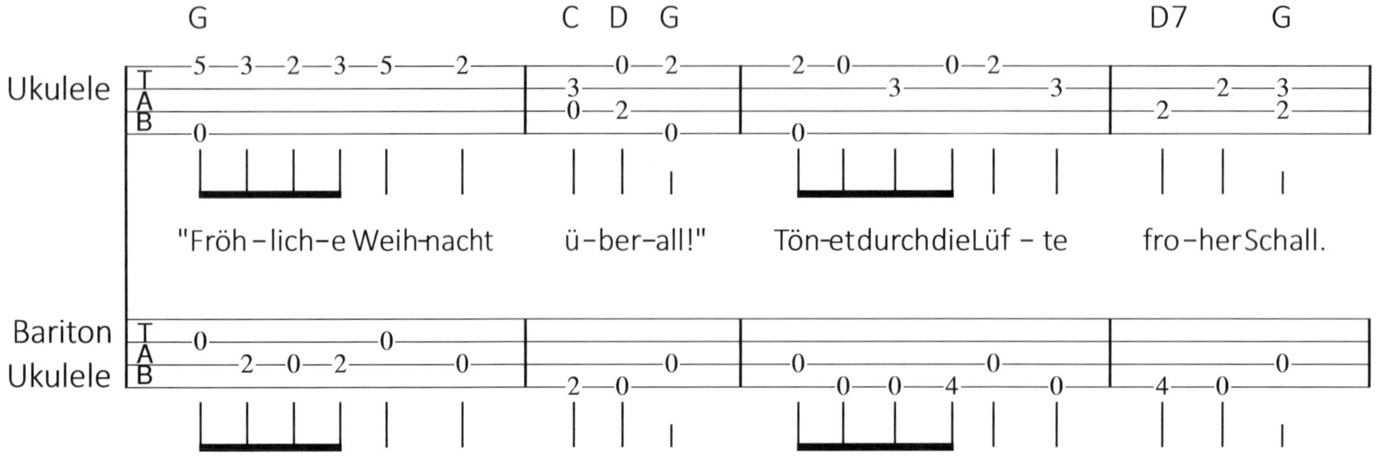

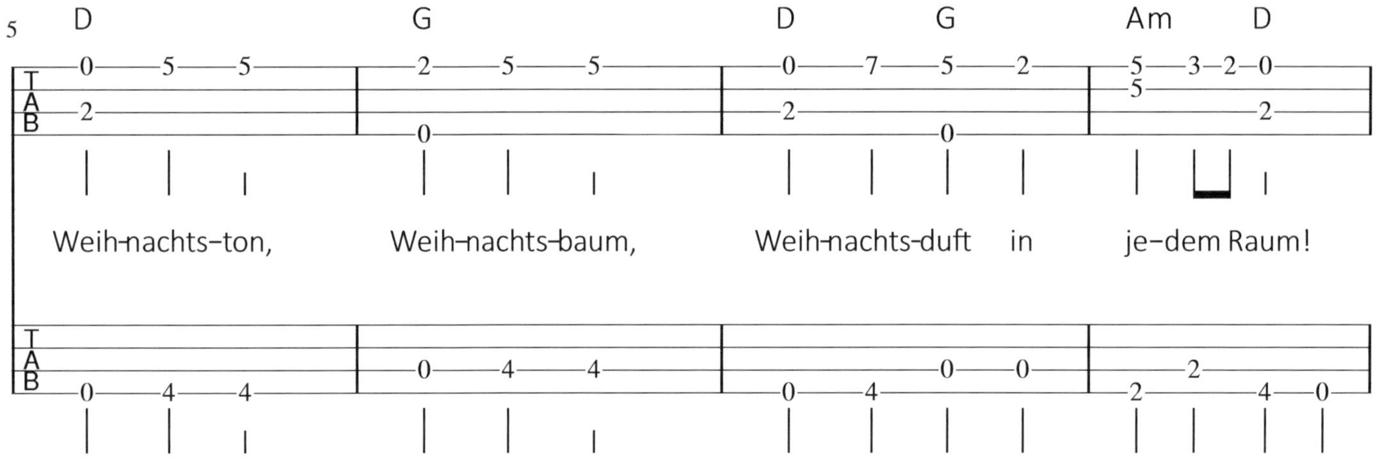

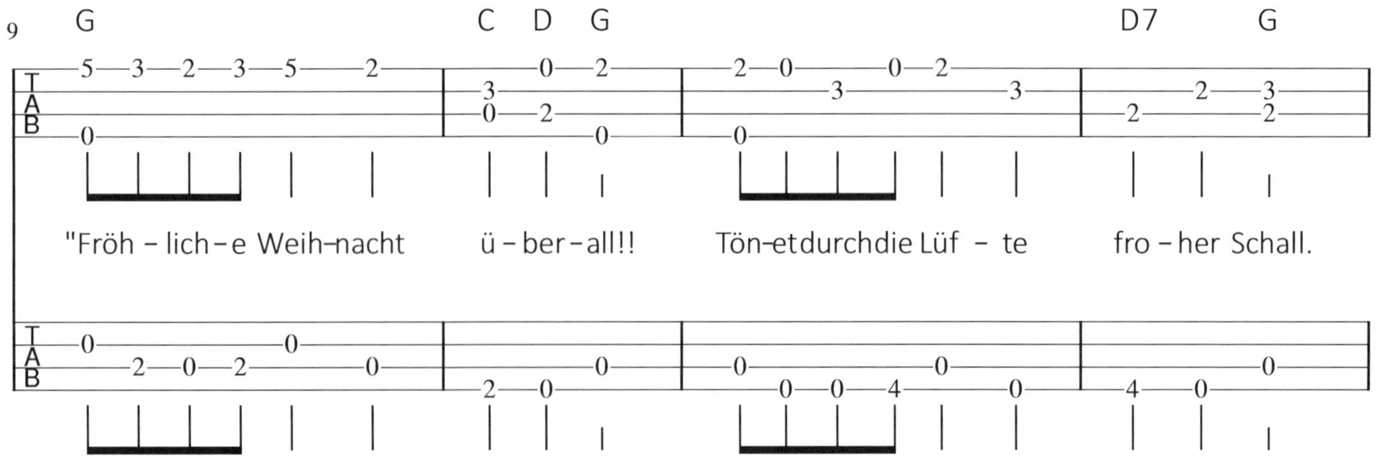

Da – rum al – le stim – met ein in den Ju – bel – ton,

denn es kommt das Licht der Welt von des Va – ters Thron.

God rest ye merry, Gentlemen

Beat: 4/4

Traditional

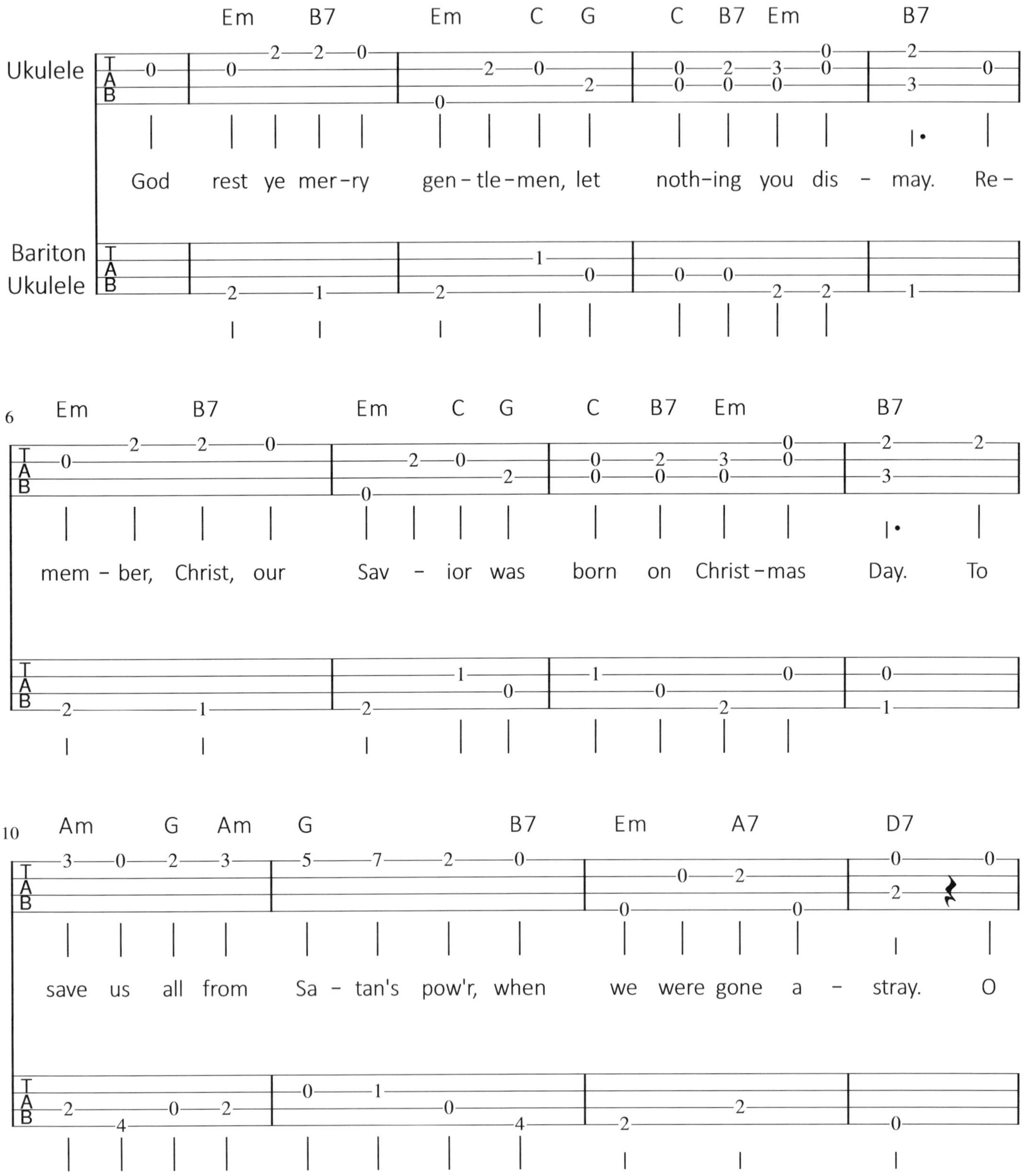

14
| G | C | G | Am | B7 | Em | | D |

ti - dings of com - fort an joy, com-fort and joy. O -

18
| G | | Em | Am | | B7 | Em |

ti - dings of com - fort and joy.

Go, tell it on the mountain

Beat: 4/4

Traditional

While shep-herds kept their watch-ing o'er Si-lent flocks by night. Be-

hold throu-out the heav-ens, there shone a ho-ly light.

Go, tell it on the moun-tain, ov-er the hills and eve-ry-whe-re. Go, tell it on the

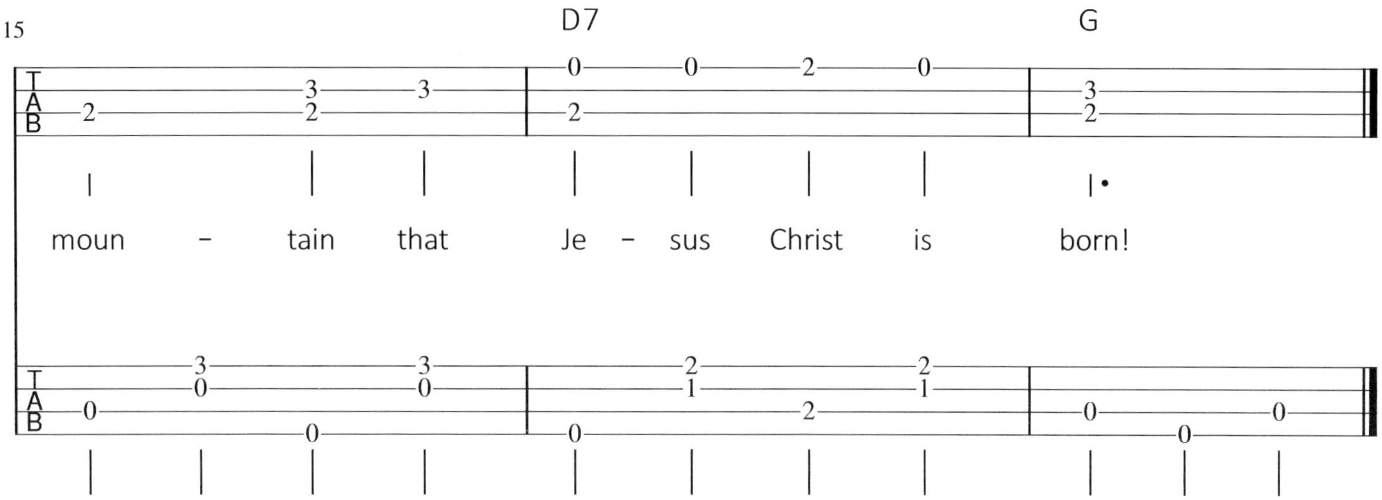
15
D7
G
TAB
moun - tain that Je - sus Christ is born!
TAB

Hark! The Herald Angels sing

Beat: 4/4

F. Mendelssohn-Bartholdy

13

C   Am E7 Am   D   G   D   G

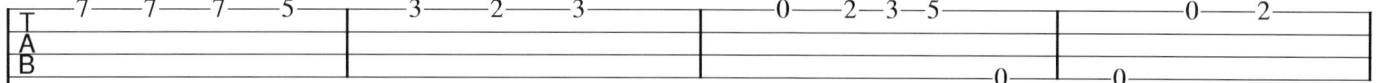

With An – gel – ic   hosts pro – claim,   "Christ is born in   Beth – le – hem.

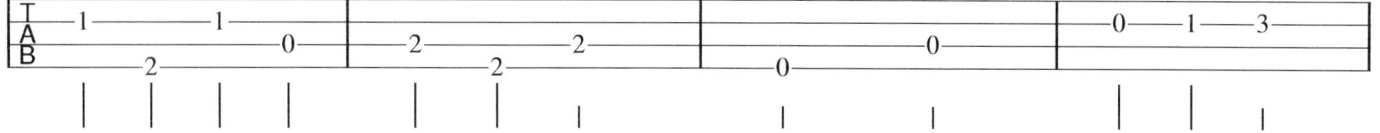

17

C   Am E7 Am   D   G   D   G

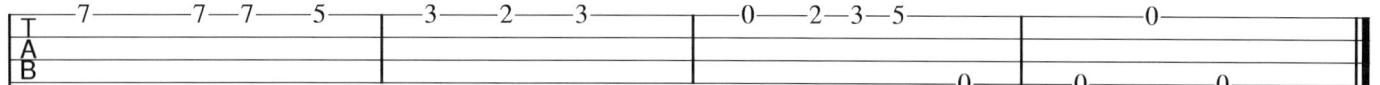

Hark! Theher – ald   an – gels sing,   Glo – ry__ to the   new–born King!"

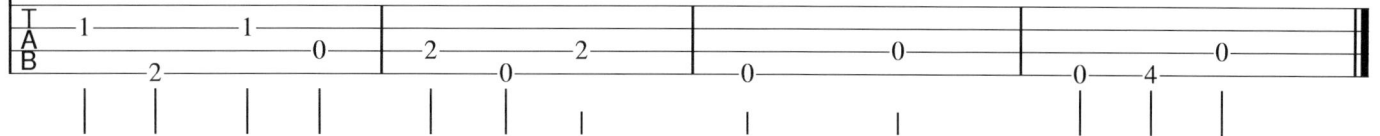

29   www.songbooks.info

Ihr Kinderlein kommet

Beat: 4/4

J. A. P. Schulz, Ch. v. Schmid

Ihr Kin – derl–ein kom – met o kom – met doch all, zur

Krip – pe her kom – met in Beth – le – hems Stall. Und

seht was in die – ser hoch – heil – ig – en Nacht, der

Vater im Himmel für Freude uns macht.

www.songbooks.info

I saw three ships

Beat: 3/4

Traditional

Ukulele / Bariton Ukulele tablature

Lyrics:
I saw three ships come sail – ing in, on
Christ – mas Day, on Christ – mas Day.
saw three ships come sail – ing in, on

14 | G | | D7 | G

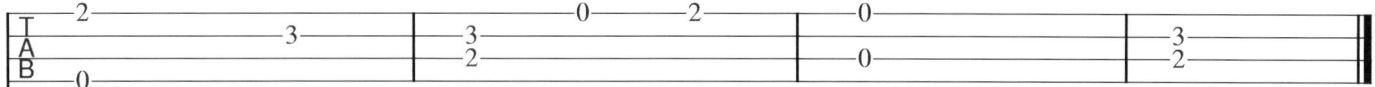

Christ – mas Day in the morn – ing.

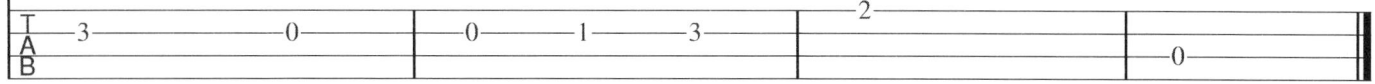

SOUNDS - ONLINE

Sämtliche Lieder wurden vertont und stehen in einem Online-Player zur Verfügung. Die Abspiel-geschwindigkeit in diesem Player ist regelbar - es ist hierfür keine Registrierung oder Software-Installation nötig.
Webadresse und Zugangsdaten (Groß- und Kleinschreibung beachten) siehe unten.

All sounds to the songs are available in an online player. The playback speed in the player can be regulated - no software installation or registration is necessary.
For the web address and access data (note upper and lower case), see below.

Webadresse/web address: www.songbooks.info/members
Benutzername/username: UkBa-Xmas
Passwort/password: UB4X8W9c

Jingle Bells

Beat: 4/4

Traditional

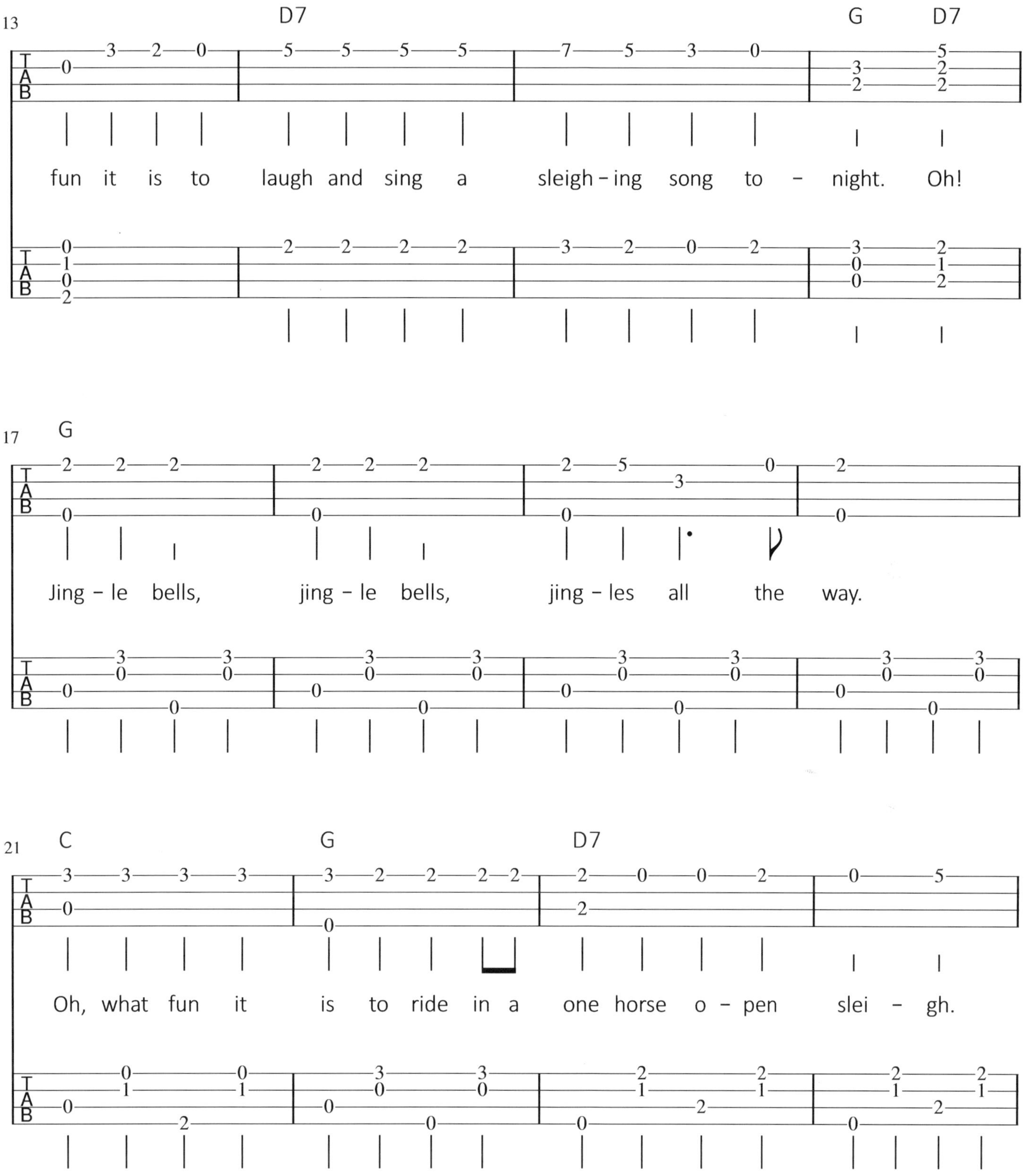
13
D7
G D7
fun it is to laugh and sing a sleigh – ing song to – night. Oh!
17
G
Jing – le bells, jing – le bells, jing – les all the way.
21
C
G
D7
Oh, what fun it is to ride in a one horse o – pen slei – gh.

25 G

Jing – le bells, jing – le bells, jing – le all the way.

29 C G D7 G

Oh, what fun it is to ride in a one horse o – pen sleigh.

Lasst uns froh und munter sein

Beat: 4/4

Traditional

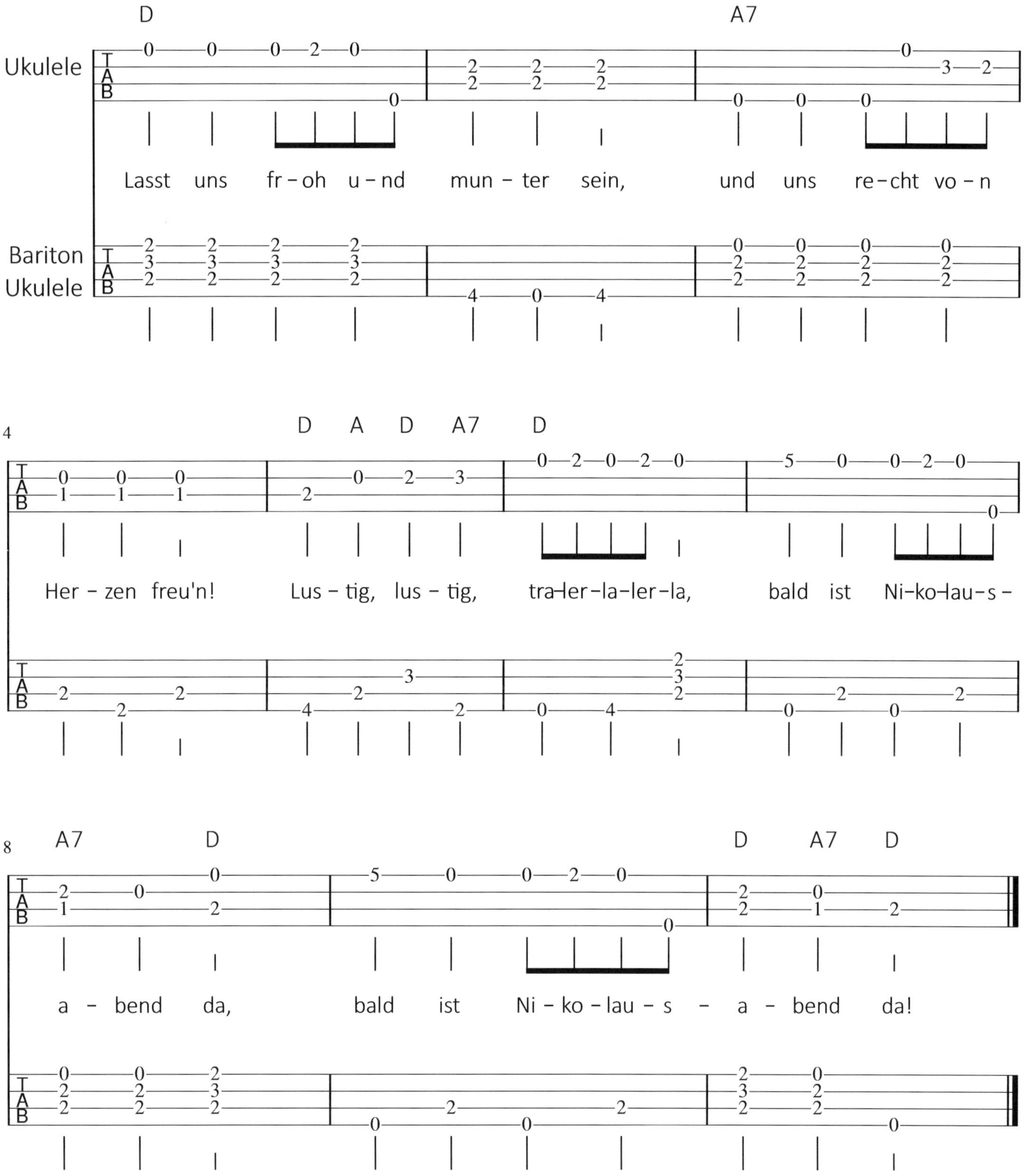

Josef, lieber Josef mein

Beat: 3/4

Traditional

Jo – sef, lie – ber Jo – sef mein,

hilf mir wie – gen mein Kind – e – lein.

Gott, der wird dein Loh – ner sein im

13 C Dm G7

Him – mel – reich, der Jung – frau Sohn Ma –

17 C

ri – a.

Kommet, ihr Hirten

Beat: 3/4

K. Riedel, Traditional

Kom - met,__ ihr - Hir - ten,__ ihr - Män - ner__ und - Frau'n,

Kom - met,__ das - lieb - li - che Kind - lein__ zu schaun!

Chris - tus, der Herr, ist heu - te ge-bo-ren, den Gott zum Hei-land euch hat er-kor-en.

G   D   G

```
T--5--------2---5-----0-----2-----
A---------------------------------
B----------------------------0-----
```

Fürch   –   tet_____   euch   nicht!

```
T--------------------------------
A--------------------------------
B--0---------------0-----0-------
```

Leise rieselt der Schnee

Beat: 3/4

E. Ebel, Traditional

Lei – se rie – selt der Schnee,

still und starr ruht der See.

Weih – nacht – lich glän – zet der Wald,

Am   D7   G

freu – e   dich,   s'Christ – kind   kommt   bald!

Maria durch ein Dornwald ging

Beat: 4/4

Traditional

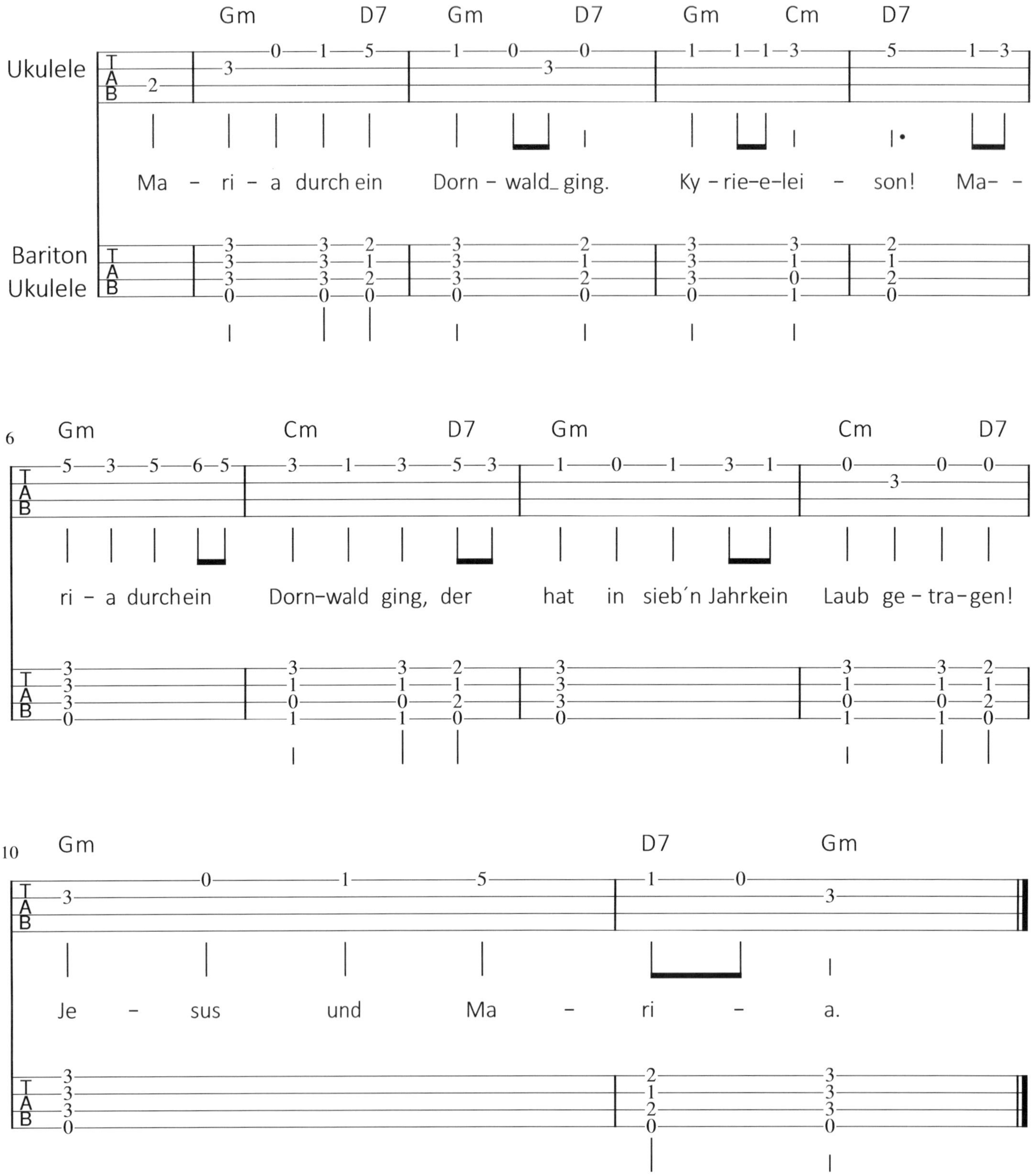

Morgen, Kinder, wirds was geben

Beat: 4/4

C. G. Hering

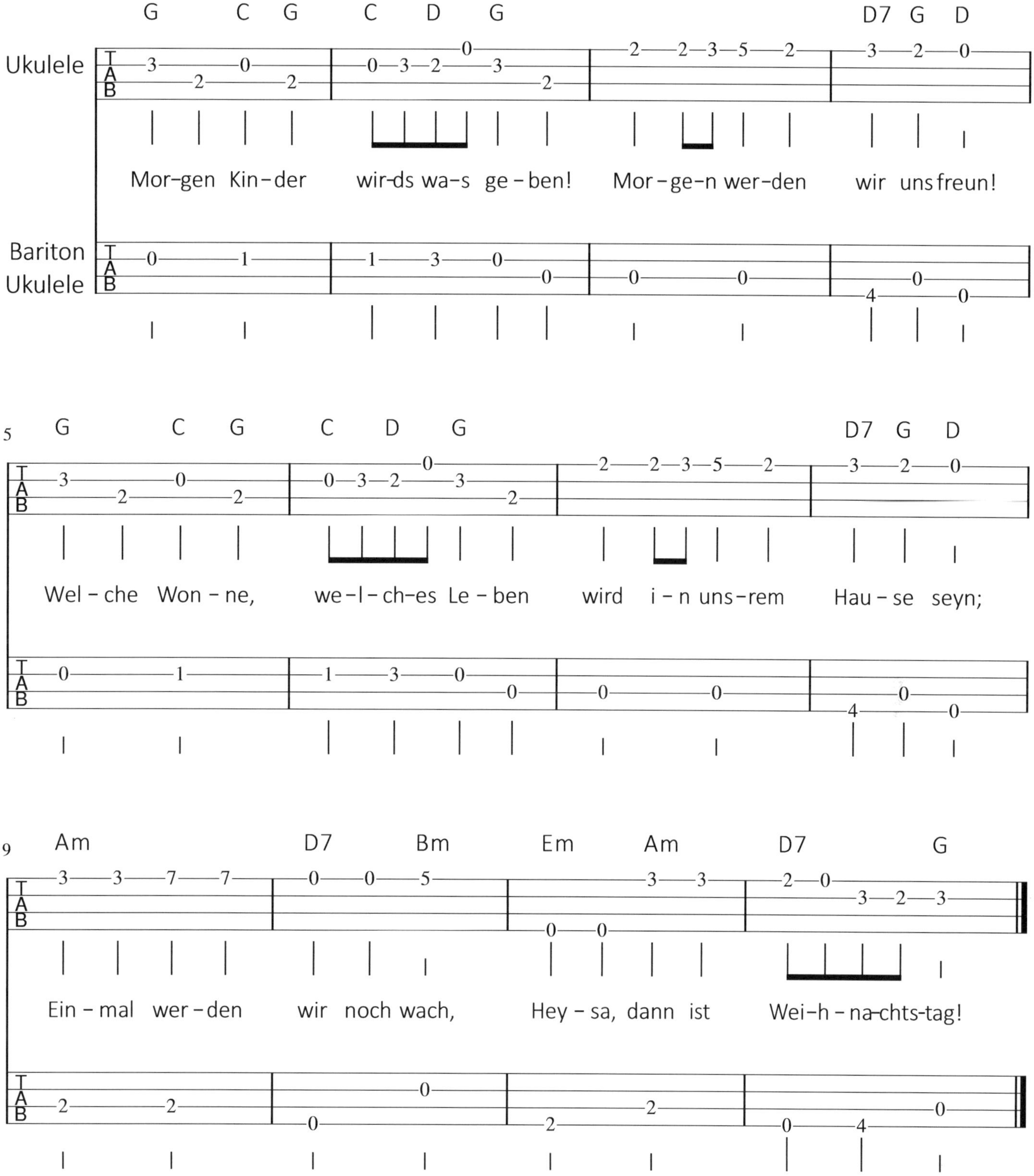

Morgen kommt der Weihnachtsmann

Beat: 4/4

W. A. Mozart

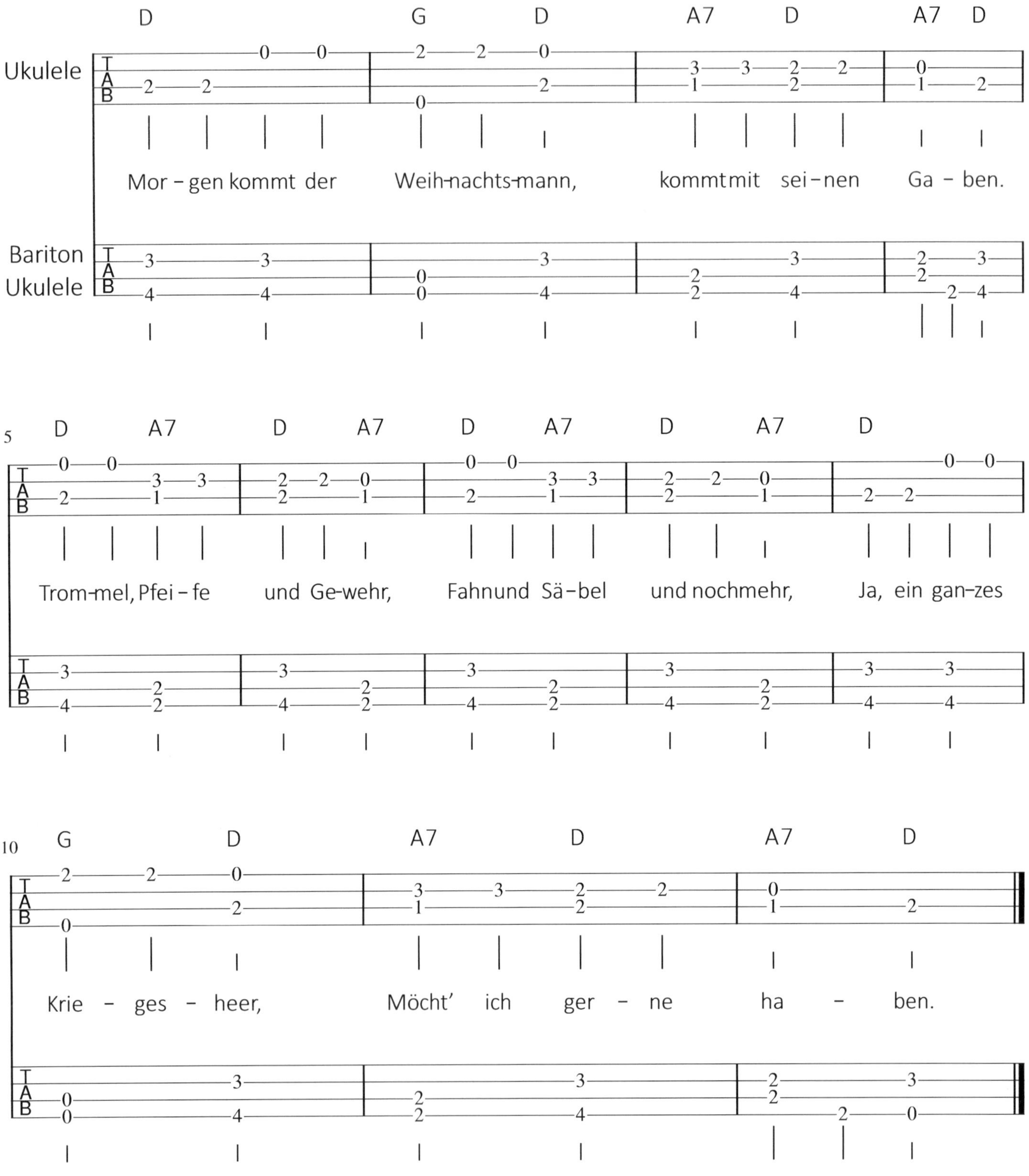

O Tannenbaum

Beat: 3/4

Traditional

O come, all ye faithful

Beat: 4/4

Traditional

14

G   D7   G   D7   G   D   G

come let us a – dore Him, O   come let us a – dore Him, O

18

C   A7   D   G   C   G   D7   G

come let us a – dore Him,   Christ the   Lord.

O du fröhliche

Beat: 4/4

J. D. Falk, Traditional

Ukulele / Bariton Ukulele tablature

Lyrics:
O du fröh - li-ch - e, o du se - li-g - e,
gra - den - bring - en - de Weih - nachts - zeit!
We - lt ging ver - lo - ren, Chri - st ist ge - bo - ren:

Freu – e – freu – e dich o Chris – ten – heit!

Stille Nacht

Beat: 3/4

F. X. Gruber, J. Mohr

Sti - lle Nacht! Hei - li - ge Nacht!

Al - les schläft, ein - sam wacht

nur das trau - te hoch - hei - li - ge Paar.

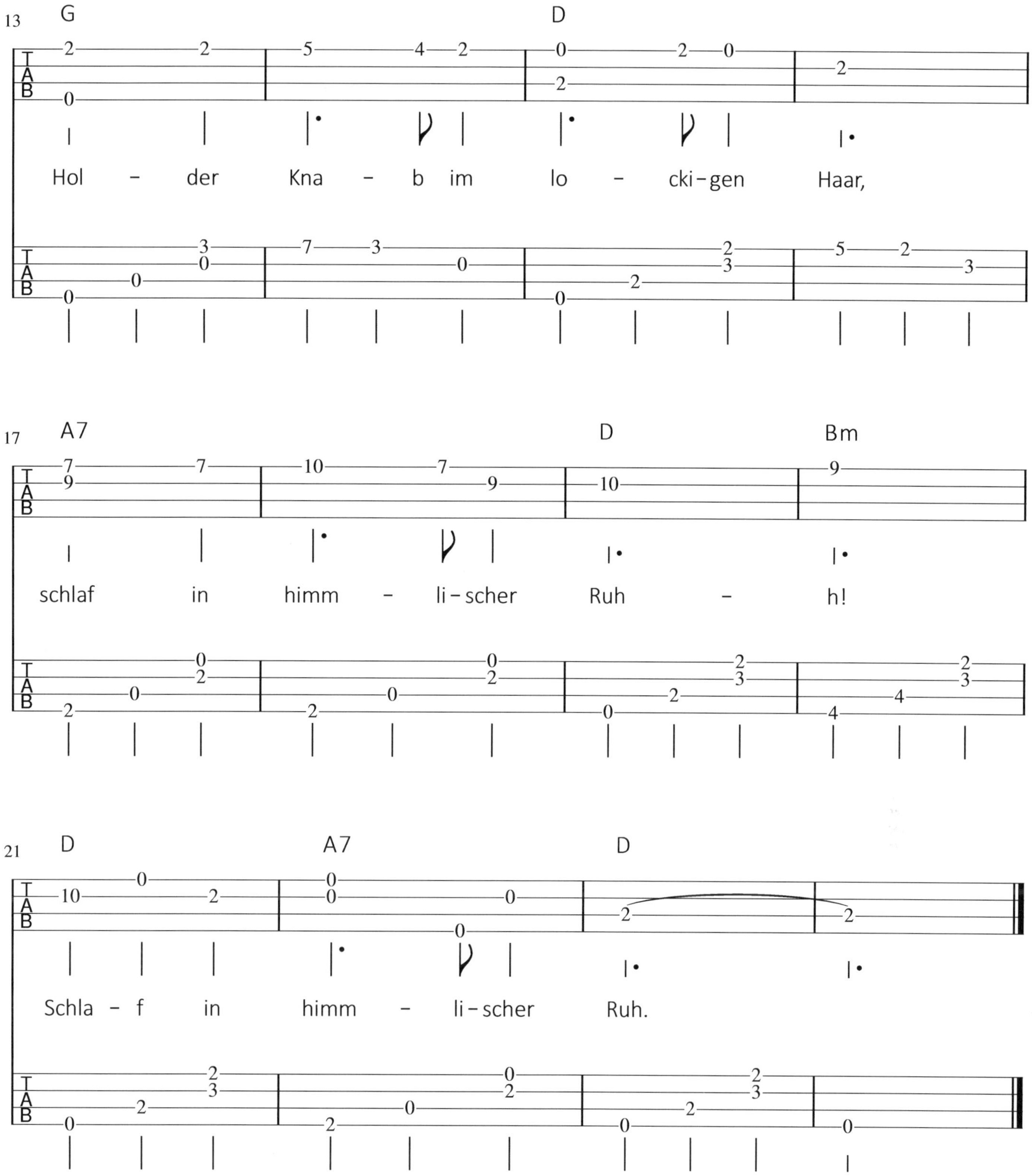
13 G D
Hol - der Kna - b im lo - cki-gen Haar,
17 A7 D Bm
schlaf in himm - li-scher Ruh - h!
21 D A7 D
Schla - f in himm - li-scher Ruh.

The first Noel

Beat: 3/4

Traditional

Lyrics:

The fi – rst No – el the an – gels did say, was to cer – tain poor shep – herds in fields as they lay. I – n fiel – ds whe – re they lay keep – ing their sheep, on a

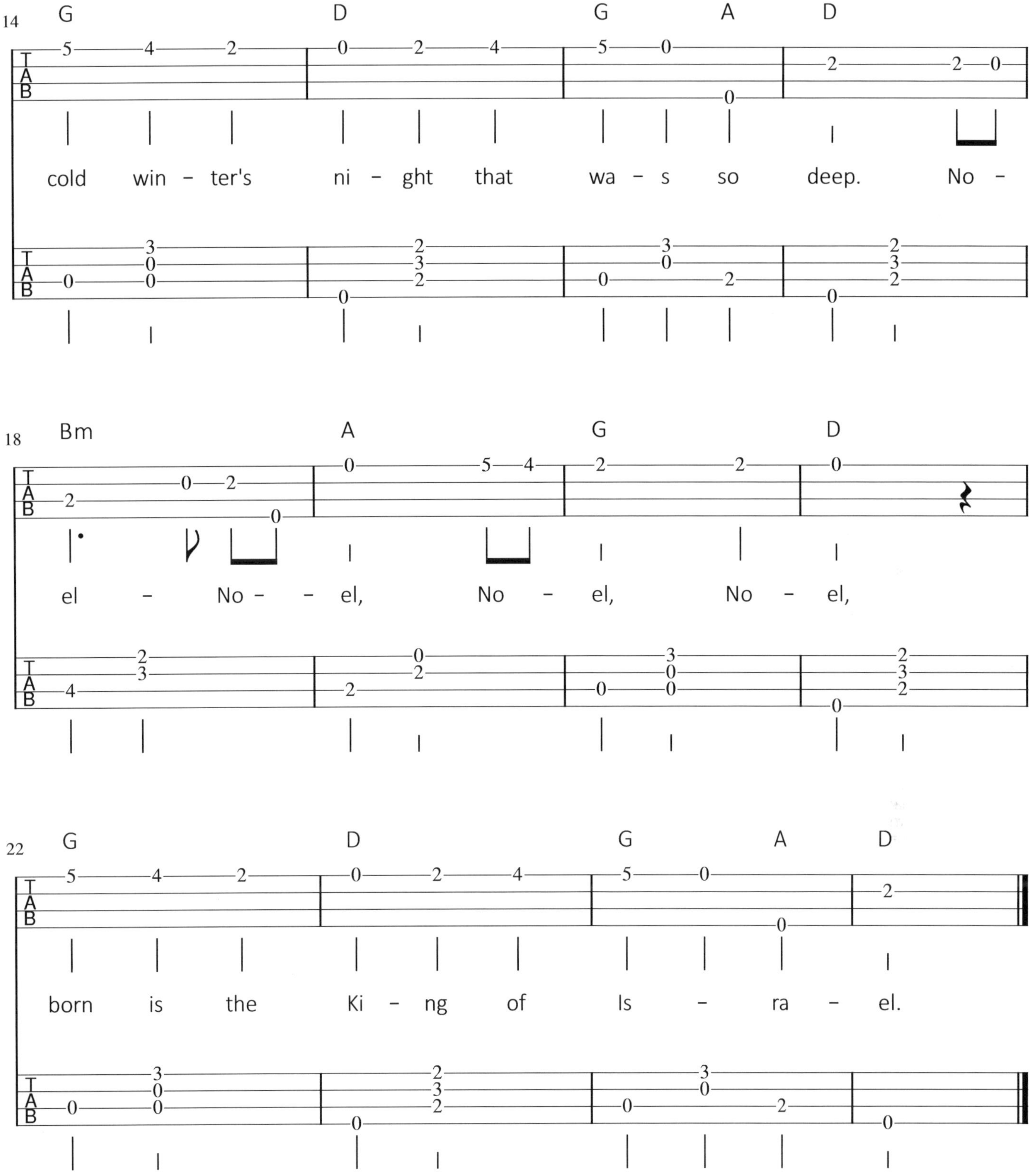
14 G D G A D
cold win – ter's ni – ght that wa – s so deep. No –
18 Bm A G D
el – No – – el, No – el, No – el,
22 G D G A D
born is the Ki – ng of Is – ra – el.

Schneeflöckchen, Weißröckchen

Beat: 3/4

H. Haberkern

Schn-ee – flöck – chen, Weiß – röck – chen, wa –nn kommst du ge –

schneit. Du wohnst in den Wol – ken, dei – n

Weg ist so weit.

Vom Himmel hoch, da komm ich her

Beat: 4/4

M. Luther, Traditional

Ukulele

| A | E | A | D | | G | A | D | | Bm | A | F♯m | Bm |

Vom Him–mel hoch da komm ich her. Ich bring' euch gu – te

Bariton Ukulele

5

| A | Em | D | | G | Em | A | | D | E | A | Bm | | F♯m | G | D | Bm |

neu – e Mär, der gu – ten Mär bring ich so viel, da – von ich sing'n und

9

| G | A | D |

sa – gen will.

We wish you a merry Christmas

Beat: 3/4

Traditional

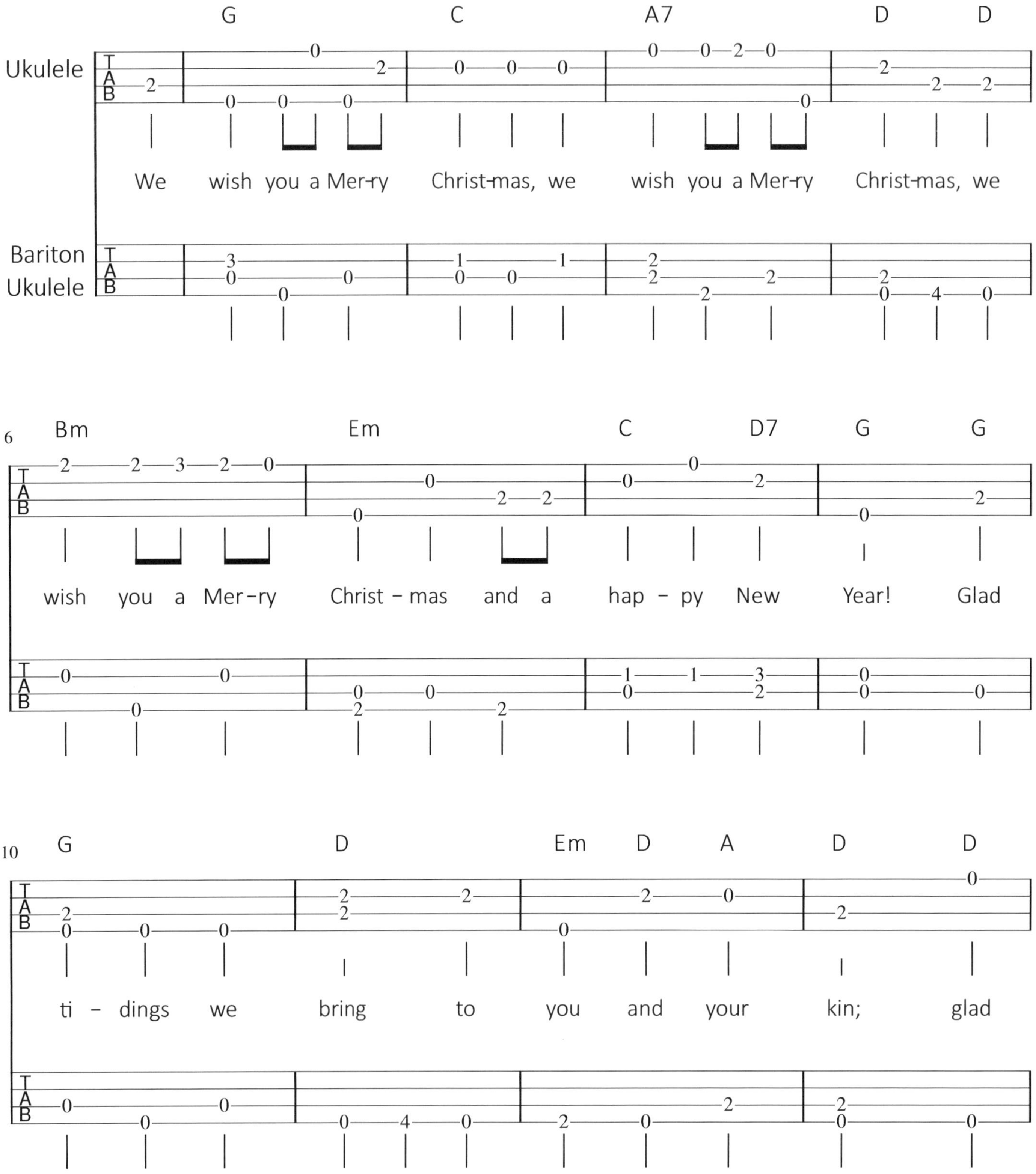

G   D   C   D   G

14

```
T|--2----0----------|--5----------------|-------------0----|-------3---||
A|------------------|--2----2----2----2-|--0----------2----|-------0---||
B|--0---------0-----|-------------------|--0----------2----|--0----0---||
```

ti – dings   for   Christ – mas   and a   hap – py   New   Year!

```
T|------------------|-------------------|--1----1----3----|--3--------||
A|--0---------0-----|-------------------|-----------------|--0--------||
B|------0-----------|--0----4----0------|-----------------|--0--------||
```

Mehr Bücher aus dieser Serie / more books of this series:

play UKULELE
Duets for Ukulele and Baritone Ukulele
20 pieces from the „Notebook of Anna Magdalena Bach"
Tabs & Online Sounds

play UKULELE
41 arrangements of Evergreens
Tabs & Online Sounds

play UKULELE
41 arrangements of classical music
Book #2
Tabs & Online Sounds

play UKULELE
41 Bearbeitungen deutscher Volkslieder
Deutsch & English
Tabs & Online Sounds

play UKULELE
18 Tango, Salsa & more
Tabs & Online Sounds

play UKULELE
38 Bearbeitungen von Liedern aus dem Mittelalter
Arrangements of songs from the Middle Ages
Deutsch & English
Tabs & Online Sounds

play UKULELE
41 arrangements of traditional music
Book #2
Deutsch & English
Tabs & Online Sounds

play UKULELE
41 arrangements of traditionals from Ireland & Great Britain
Deutsch & English
Tabs & Online Sounds

play UKULELE
9 BEARBEITUNGEN VON LIEDERN VON JOHANN STRAUSS SOHN
ARRANGEMENTS OF SONGS BY JOHANN STRAUSS SOHN
Deutsch & English
Tabs & Online Sounds

Made in the USA
Middletown, DE
08 October 2024